KV-373-793

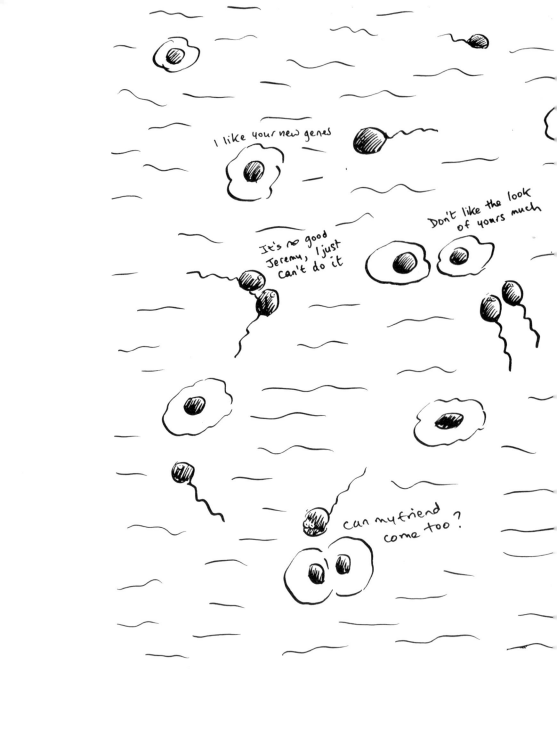

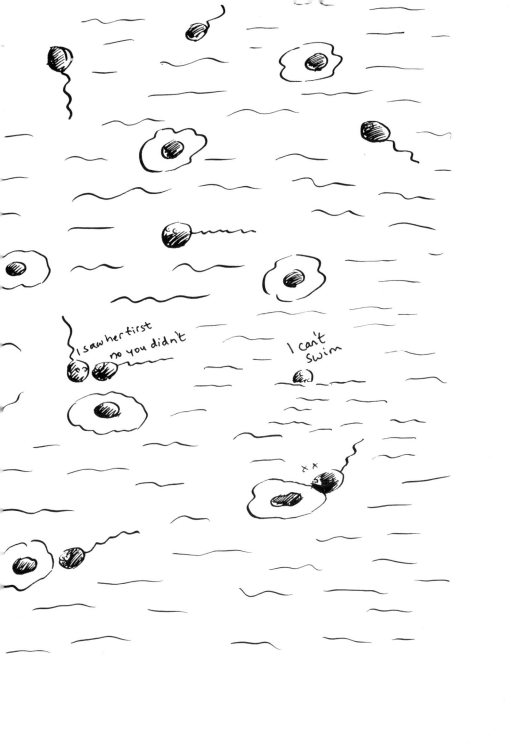

Richard Huggett is an actor, author and playwright. His TV credits include *Dr Finlay's Casebook* and *Crossroads*, and he has appeared in the feature films *Goodbye Mr Chips* and *The Colditz Story*. He has recently completed two new plays, *The First Night of Macbeth* about Shakespeare, and *Weekend with Willie* about Somerset Maugham. He is currently writing the official biography of Binkie Beaumont.

Richard Huggett

Bedside Sex

Illustrations by
Susan Hellard

Fontana/Collins

Happily dedicated to
Richard Lamb and Sue Lamb
whose unspeakably filthy sense of humour
enlivened many evenings and has greatly
enriched this book

First published by Quartet Books
under the title *The Wit and Humour of Sex* 1975
This new edition first issued by Fontana Paperbacks 1985

Copyright © Richard Huggett, 1975, 1985

Set in Linotron Pilgrim

Made and printed in Great Britain by
William Collins Sons & Co. Ltd, Glasgow

Conditions of Sale
This book is sold subject to the condition
that it shall not, by way of trade or otherwise,
be lent, re-sold, hired out or otherwise circulated
without the publisher's prior consent in any form of
binding or cover other than that in which it is
published and without a similar condition
including this condition being imposed
on the subsequent purchaser

Contents

Acknowledgements

The following people have all contributed something funny to this book, and I offer them my most grateful thanks.

Richard Lamb
John Gale
Kenneth McClellan
Magdalen Egerton
Michael Letchford
David Belcher
Charles Burbridge
Diana Ashcroft
Brendan Behan
Arthur St George Huggett
Roger Woddis
Kenneth Tynan
Cardew Robinson
Mark Stuart
Peter Bull
David Bolt
Katherine Whitehorn
Roland Gant
Diana Lambert
Theresa Ford
Harry Talor-Chambray
Jock Henderson
Richard Gordon
Mrs Rosemary Macomber
Allan Aspin
Mark Blythe

Mary Gill
Fred Horton
Mrs D. Bentley
Robin Stanley Sanford Thompson
Ray Minshull
Christopher Raeburn
George Ross
Paul Bura
Peter Innocent
Graham Wiremu
Anthony Jay
Michael Rubinstein
The Editor of the *New Statesman*
Robert Morley
Peter Lee-Wright
Patricia Samuels
The Editor of the *Guardian*
Bob Smith
Stan Rigby
Michael Jeanes
Alan Roger Davis
   and Kenny Challoner
   of the Berwick Market
Charles Collinwood
Barry Humphreys
Joe Wiebkin

Gentlemen on Sex

Sexual intercourse is a grossly overrated pastime: the position is undignified, the pleasure momentary, and the consequences utterly damnable.

Lord Chesterfield

To my mind this is the perfect sexual witticism – succinct, elegantly phrased and very funny. I once told it to a former publisher and his associates (male) at lunch. They all laughed loudly. But when the laughter had died away they sighed and said quietly, almost with one voice, 'Oh, God, it's so *true.*' I thought this was very sad.

Bedside Sex

I've got three kids – one of each.

Sex doesn't bother me, I guess it's here to stay.

Groucho Marx

It must be admitted that the English have sex on the brain, which is a *frightfully* uncomfortable place to have it.

Malcolm Muggeridge

Gentlemen on Sex

On the continent they have sex. In England they have hot water bottles.

George Mikes

Sir Thomas Beecham

He hated women in the orchestra and was particularly irritated by a very famous lady cellist who came to play a concerto. During the rehearsals he contained himself as well as he could, but finally burst out, '*Madam, you have God's greatest gift of nature in between your legs and all you can do is to scratch it!*'

One day an unfamiliar face appeared in the flute section.
'I don't think we've met,' said Sir Thomas charmingly.
The man promptly stood up.
'No, Sir Thomas, I'm new today.'
'What is your name, my dear sir?'
'Ball, Sir Thomas, Ball.'
'Ball, eh?' replied Beecham. 'Ball? . . . hmmm . . . how very *singular!*'

The famous German lyric soprano, Marta Fuchs, was under serious consideration for a new production of *Tosca* which Sir Thomas Beecham was due to conduct at Covent Garden. As he had never heard her, he sent a talent scout (male) to Berlin to hear and report. A telegram arrived with a somewhat predictable spelling mistake. MARTA FUCKS WONDERFUL. Beecham's reply was swift. I'M SURE SHE DOES AND I'M GLAD YOU'RE ENJOYING YOURSELF BUT CAN SHE SING TOSCA?

Bedside Sex

The reputation for chastity is useful to a woman – and chastity has its uses also.

La Rochefoucauld

Three sayings attributed to Confucius:

Resist your aggressor, but if rape is inevitable, then lie back and enjoy it.

Rape is impossible because a woman with her skirts up can run quicker than a man with his trousers down.

Saving candles by going to bed early is a false economy if the result is twins.

Dr Joad was severely reprimanded by Lord Reith for quoting this last on *The Brains Trust*.

Gentlemen on Sex

Sexual fidelity is not necessary to a well-conducted marriage. Your eldest son should certainly be your own, but beyond this it is excessively vulgar to enquire too closely into the paternity of your children.

Simon Raven

When asked 'Is sex dirty?' Woody Allen is said to have replied:

Yes, if it's done right.

Bedside Sex

Cedric Hardwicke was once asked by a TV interviewer if being bald made a man extra virile. His famous reply was:

Possibly, but it gives a man fewer chances of proving it.

When a man says he has had pleasure with a woman, he does not mean conversation or tea.

Dr Johnson

Table d' Hôte

Gentlemen on Sex

What men call gallantry, and gods adultery,
Is much more common where the climate's sultry.

Lord Byron

Sir Herbert Beerbohm Tree was the First Gentleman of the
theatre and a great lover of women. He scattered his maker's
image over the West End with enormous enthusiasm, thus
enriching not only the theatre but also the post-war cinema.
It was during the very successful run of *Julius Caesar* that he

visited one of his women. He undressed and she commented admiringly on his physical splendour. He politely spurned the compliment, saying: '*I have come to bury Caesar, not to praise him.*'

James Thurber
I love the idea of there being *two* sexes, don't you?

Women, observing that their mates went out of their way to make themselves agreeable, rightly surmised that sex had something to do with it. From that she logically surmised that sex was recreational rather than procreational. The small, hardy band of girls who failed to get this point were responsible for the popularity of women's field hockey.

Is sex necessary?

There are three sexes: men, women and clergymen.

Voltaire

There are four sexes: men, women, clergymen and journalists.

W. Somerset Maugham

If you wish to rid yourself of a difficult and time-wasting woman, then you must concentrate on her bad points and freedom will once again be yours.

Ovid

Gentlemen on Sex

When we men want to, then women don't. But when we don't then they want to exceedingly.

Terence

Lust is an enemy to the purse, a foe to the conscience, a canker to the mind, a corrosive to the person, a weakness to the wit, a besotter to the senses and finally a mortal bane to all the body.

Pliny

Charlton Heston is the only bloke I've ever met who makes me feel like a pouf.

A famous boxing champion

H. G. Wells once boasted that he couldn't write unless he'd had sexual intercourse after breakfast, after lunch and after dinner. 'That's v-v-v-very interesting,' said Somerset Maugham, 'and what do you do after t-t-t-tea?'

Two Englishmen arrive at a railway station, one to leave by train, the other to see him off after a weekend. 'Thanks frightfully, old man,' says the first from inside the train, 'jolly decent of you, splendid time,' etc.

'Not a bit, old man,' says the second, 'jolly nice to see you again, enjoyed the weekend myself,' etc.

As the train started to leave the first said, 'Oh, by the way, your wife is jolly good in bed,' and sat down. An Irishman in the corner said, 'Excuse me sorrr, but was I hearing you say that his wife was jolly good in bed?'

'That's right,' replied the Englishman, 'you see, he's an old friend of mine and I didn't want to hurt him.'

Ladies on Sex

Mae West

'What do you think of sex?' was a routine question at press conferences. Her invariable reply was 'We have a lot in common. In a manner of speaking and in my usual modest way, I can claim to have invented it.'

'How tall are you?' she asked an outsize cowboy in the film *Myra Breckenridge*. 'Six foot seven and a half inches,' he replied proudly. 'Forget about the six foot, honey,' she replied looking him up and down, 'let's just talk about the seven and a half inches.'

In the early thirties she sent a telegram to Bernard Shaw.

'What do you want for Christmas? Whisky, cigars or what, Mae West.'

The reply from England was swift.

'Don't drink, don't smoke, yours G.B.S.'

The best way to enjoy sex is standing up in a hammock.

Is that a pistol in your pants, honey, or are you just pleased to see me?

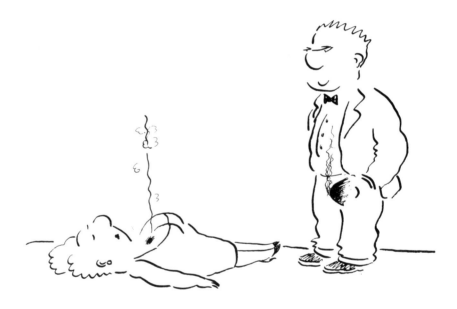

Mrs Patrick Campbell

Marriage is the deep, deep peace of the double-bed after the hurly-burly of the *chaise-longue*.

Ladies on Sex

About her second husband, George Cornwallis-West:
    George is a *golden* man; six foot four
    and everything in proportion.

When she was warned that a couple in her company were
having an affair and probably sleeping together:
    I don't care what people do as long as they don't do it in the
    street and frighten the horses.

It must be the mating season again

Lady Tree
Sir Herbert Beerbohm Tree's philandering was well known in
the profession and tolerated with extraordinary patience and
understanding by his witty and sensible wife. To young girls
joining the company Lady Tree would invariably say:
    Now don't forget, girls. Be careful of Sir Herbert. It starts
    with a compliment and ends with a confinement.

She herself had three daughters spaced out at seven-year
intervals. When her friends asked her why there were such

large gaps between her pregnancies, she shrugged her shoulders and said, '*Well, my dear, I suppose I must wait my turn.*'

Tallulah Bankhead

She had a deep husky voice which was one of her principal attractions. One day she was interviewed by a male journalist whose voice was high and squeaky. 'Miss Bankhead, do you ever get mistaken for a man on the telephone?' he asked.

'Never, honey,' she replied promptly. 'Do you?'

During her years in England in the dizzy twenties, she had a tumultuous love affair with a very blue-blooded young gentleman. The family disapproved and succeeded in breaking up the affair and getting him engaged to a girl of similar background and aspirations. The two families were dining at the Savoy Grill when Tallulah appeared. She walked past their table and greeted her former lover very pleasantly but he ignored her. So she went up to him and said for all the two families to hear: '*What's the matter, darling, don't you recognize me with my clothes on?*'

Dorothy Parker

If all the girls from Columbia University were laid from end to end, I wouldn't be a bit surprised.

When she found herself pregnant and unmarried:
It's like putting all your eggs into one bastard.

To a famous actress who had announced over the years a great many false pregnancies and miscarriages and who finally astonished everybody by actually having a baby:

Congratulations, darling, we always knew you had it in you.

When somebody gave her a canary:

I call him Onan because he's always spilling his seed.

25

Katherine Whitehorn

Never sleep with anybody whose troubles are worse than your own.

Never take anyone to bed in the afternoon: someone better is bound to turn up later.

Never take a girl to bed on the first date – she'll expect it and therefore be disappointed.

Sex is good when you can have any man you want, and bad when any man who wants can have you.

Advice to men from the *Observer*:
   Never, but *never*, smile in a public lavatory.

Her articles in the *Observer* on the British expatriate community in Tangier contained two gems:

   One genuine vice remains in force in Tangier – there have always been plenty of Moroccans prepared to give quite a new meaning to the phrase 'a gentleman's gentleman'.

   For those who are prepared to dismiss Tangier as Queensville-by-sea, it is a surprise to find that it is not so much wicked as desperately *respectable*!

Sex is like medicine – nasty at first but it does you good.

Anna Pavlova

Ladies on Sex

An English woman's bed is her castle.

Lady Castlerosse

Are you in the National Truss?

Two typists chatting in the typing pool.
  'That new bloke, Mr Davies, doesn't he dress well?'
  'Yes, and quickly too.'

Help! I've just been raped by a coal miner.
  How did you know it was a coal miner?
  Because I did all the work.

The husband returns home and says to his wife, 'I've just heard that the milkman has had every woman in the street except one.'

The wife thought for a moment: 'I expect it's that snooty, standoffish bitch from number 46. Nothing and nobody's good enough for *her*.'

The woman rushed into a police station. 'Help! I've been graped.'

'I think you mean "raped" madam,' said the sergeant.

'No,' she said, 'they were a bunch.'

Sex in and around Westminster

Graffito in the gentlemen's lavatory in the House of Commons:
YOU HAVE THE FUTURE OF THE WHOLE WORLD IN YOUR
HANDS.

Graffito seen in El Vino's loo:
    MARGARET THATCHER FOR P.M.
and somebody had written underneath:
    WHY NOT A.M.?

When Guy Burgess took up his first diplomatic post in
Washington his reputation for drink, tactless behaviour and

unashamed homosexuality preceded him. The Ambassador gave him a stern lecture on his arrival, stressing that an irreproachably high standard of moral and social behaviour was expected of him. He also warned him that the racial situation in America was unusually tense and that American susceptibilities were not to be offended in this matter. Burgess listened with an amused and sardonic tolerance. 'What you really mean, sir,' he finally said, 'is that I mustn't fuck Paul Robeson.'

MR PITT: Sir, you will either be hanged or die by the pox.
MR WILKES: Sir, that depends on whether I embrace your principles or your mistress.

Christopher Soames, English Ambassador in Paris, was attempting to explain the peculiarities of our parliamentary system to some French friends. The appellation 'Chief Whip' presented problems, and the French friends had their worst suspicions about the English character fully confirmed when this was translated as '*le premier flagellationst*'.

Scurrility, in song or pamphlet, which added so much life and colour to eighteenth-century and nineteenth-century politics, is happily not totally absent from the contemporary scene.

Sex in and around Westminster

During a recent march of industrial strikers through the City and West End of London to Downing Street, a very scurrilous song was being good-humouredly chanted by many thousands of cheerful young strikers. It dealt with the minority sexual tastes of a prominent political personage who will be discreetly referred to as John Smith, and it was sung to the tune of a popular rugby song:

Oh, John Smith he is a queer
John Smith he is a queer
Eee-yi-yippy-yi,
John Smith he is a queer.

There were many verses of even greater scurrility. A policeman was standing in Fleet Street watching the strikers pass and was convulsed with laughter as he listened to the song. Noticing this, a passing cyclist approached him. 'Would this be regarded as defamation, slander or fair comment?' he asked. The policeman shook his head and grinned. 'None of those things, sir,' he replied. 'I think it would be regarded as a contravention of the Official Secrets Act!'

Bedside Sex

PRIME MINISTER (addressing the House): Now what shall I do about this Homosexual Bill?
VOICE FROM THE OPPOSITION: Pay it.

Ancient showbiz joke

When it comes to high-ranking, top-level sex scandals there is no doubt that – to the jealous admiration of France and America – England reigns supreme. With the Profumo affair in 1964, the twentieth century shows that she has not lost her grip. Happily, the public decided to treat it as an enormous joke, and witticisms about Profumo, Stephen Ward, Mandy Rice-Davies and other glamorous ladies became compulsory small-talk at parties. It was said that President Kennedy was unable to talk business with the British Ambassador until he'd heard the latest Profumo joke. Since they were sexual rather than political, this book is clearly the right place for them.

It was inevitable that the lustful Jamaican whose violent passions started the affair should have been known as MASTER OF THE BLACK ROD and THE CHIEF WHIP, and imaginary headlines about one of the ladies of the affair – LAST SEEN AT LONDON AIRPORT UNDER A VISCOUNT and RECENTLY SIGHTED AT BRIGHTON UNDER A PEER – filled the gossip columns.

A typical fiction of the affair has the lady in the case in bed, suddenly the Man in the Mask enters and climbs into bed with her. When he has finished he gets up and moves to the door.

'Thank you very much, Mr Macmillan,' she says.

'Oh dear, oh dear,' stammers the man, 'how *did* you know it was me?'

'Easily,' she says. 'I've never had it so good.'

Sex scandals, it seems, come once every ten years. If Profumo and Stephen Ward belong to the sixties, then it is undoubtedly those associated with another lady who belong to the seventies. When the story of this connection broke in the press, Lord Lambton and Lord Jellicoe had to tender their immediate resignations from the government. The lady had strong political views and gave her favours, it appeared, only to the Conservatives:

I don't travel steerage,
I always go Burke's Peerage.
Tories are a girl's best friends.

It was reported that two judges in their club were discussing the matter:

FIRST JUDGE: I think it should have been handled better.
SECOND JUDGE: And so it jolly well should, at £50 a time.

One Conservative MP observed wistfully:

'If only it could have been Ted, it would have done us *so* much good.'

Another Conservative MP who had been a colleague of Profumo made a lightning calculation of her rates and said:

Bedside Sex

'Why, her rates are even lower than those of Jack's girl. Isn't
that a remarkable triumph of the counter-inflation policy?'

Sex in and around Westminster

A call-girl racket to supply sex to visiting foreigners whom Her Majesty's Government wished to entertain and keep happy and a secret fund for the purpose were exposed at this time:

BLUE LIGHT

Time was when only Bolsheviks
Resorted to such knavish tricks
As using under-cover chicks
To check on their adherents.
Young Tories too now think it best
That women keen to serve the West
Should pass the brothelizer test
And all be given clearance.

But where to find those ladies who
Though bought and sold for what they do
Are patriotic through and through
And innocent of treason?
No need to search cheap hotels
In search of loyal Jezebels
When there are those delightful gels
Who decorate the season.

Roger Woddis, *New Statesman*

One day Winston Churchill was making an impassioned speech in the House of Commons. Suddenly Mr Attlee saw from the Opposition bench that he had his fly-buttons undone. He tried to signal this to Churchill but without success – he was too involved in his speech to notice any interruptions. Attlee scribbled a brief message on a piece of paper and sent it down the Opposition bench. It was taken across the floor by the messenger, travelled down the Government bench and eventually finished in Anthony Eden's hands. He paled and tried to get Churchill's attention by tugging his coat. Useless. He tugged harder. Eventually Churchill stopped in mid-sentence and said testily: 'Well, Anthony, what is it?'

'Sir, your fly-buttons are undone.'

'Well, what of it?' was the impatient answer, 'dead bird can't fly out of nest.'

A debate in the House of Lords on the difficulty of taxing the oldest profession produced the following:

LORD BEAUMONT: Is it true that income tax is not levied on the earnings of prostitutes, and if so, why?

LORD ABERDARE: The profits of prostitutes are liable to income tax. Whenever a case comes to the notice of the Inland Revenue, they are assessed for tax.

LADY GAITSKELL: Would it not be possible to charge the clients VAT?

LORD ABERDARE: That would depend on the turnover (laughter).

LORD TENBY: Does that mean the Government would be living on immoral earnings?

LORD ABERDARE: No, it merely means that under Schedule D, all trade activities are taxable. And under Schedule D you are allowed to set off expenses against your profits (loud laughter).

Hansard

Bedside Sex

Lady Summerskill (Labour) said 'I heard somebody laugh but I wonder if the peer who laughed has ever been to a birth-control clinic where there is a big black-bearded man? Now is a big black-bearded man the right person to teach twelve-year-old girls about the most intimate thing in their lives?'

Lord Brown (Labour): 'You are ignoring the amendment. We are not concerned with who teaches the subject.'

Lady Summerskill retorted: 'You know very little about sex. I have known you for a long time.'

Guardian

Winston Churchill once confessed that he had had a homosexual experience with Ivor Novello. 'And what was it like?' he was asked.

'Musical,' came the swift reply.

Sex in the Hospital

We have a motto here at St Benedicts Mr Smith, LOVE THINE ENEMAS

Woman is a primitive animal who micturates once a day, defecates once a week, menstruates once a month, parturates once a year and copulates whenever she has the opportunity.

W. Somerset Maugham, quoting
a Professor of Gynaecology at
St Thomas's Hospital in
the 1890s

A man went to a hospital for a vasectomy. During the operation the surgeon's scalpel slipped and severed a testicle, so he sent the nurse to the cafeteria for an onion which he sutured in as a replacement. Some weeks later the man returned for a check-up; the surgeon asked him how he felt. 'Fine,' said the patient, 'except for one thing. *Whenever I pass a hamburger joint, I get an erection.*'

Sex in the Hospital

A woman goes into hospital to have her tenth baby and she is attended by the same doctor who has delivered the other nine. 'That's the tenth kid you've had by this man,' he says to her after the delivery. 'Why don't you marry him?'

'No, doctor, I couldn't,' she says.

'You owe it to the kids and to yourself,' he says.

'No, doctor, really I couldn't,' she whimpers in her distress.

'Well, why ever not?' he asks impatiently.

'Well, doctor,' she says, 'it's like this . . . I don't like him.'

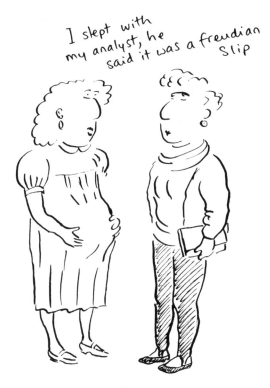

I slept with my analyst, he said it was a freudian slip

A young man goes to his doctor to see if, as he suspects, he has got AIDS. The doctor examines him and finds out that he has. 'Go to an Indian restaurant: eat three large platefuls of very hot spicy curry and then wash it down with a large spoonful of castor oil.'

'Will this cure the AIDS?' asks the young man in bewilderment.

'No, it won't,' replies the doctor, 'but it'll teach you what your arse-hole is for.'

What do you call a nurse who has a sex change?
A trans-sister.

The Professor of Physiology was lecturing his class and he had two wall-charts on display – one showing the female body and the other showing the male. He pointed to the man's penis and said to the girl in the front row: 'What is that?' The girl leapt to her feet, anxious to give the right answer. 'It's the . . . the . . .' and then her memory failed her. Snapping her fingers impatiently, she tried to remember. 'It's the . . . the . . . the . . . oh, what *is* it? . . . it's the . . . the . . . oh, hell, *I had it on the tip of my tongue last night . . . !*'

Dr Richard Gordon

Bedside Sex

My father, the late Professor Arthur Huggett, loved telling jokes. Or rather, he loved telling three jokes which were the mainstay of his comic repertoire. One had no connection with sex and therefore no place in this book, but the other two follow here. We in the family heard them many times and boredom was offset by a slight element of competition: we would add up every Christmas the times we had heard them and a small prize was given to the one with the largest score, though we were on our honour not to bring up the subject or in any way prompt him when we were in his company. In later years his memory would fail him and he would get the jokes mixed up, get the point wrong or bring in the point too soon. Here they are in their original pristine form.

The late Dr Campbell of the Glasgow Infirmary used to give a lecture to the medical school on the physiology of the penis. It was give at the end of every summer term, and since it was illustrated with coloured lantern slides it was widely attended by students from other medical schools in the city. These slides illustrated the penis from all over the world; Russia, Iceland, England, America, Japan and many African and South American tribes.

On one occasion he was addressing an unusually packed house and there was a girl who was clearly not enjoying it. She was a white-faced, tight-lipped, disapproving girl and as each slide came onto the screen she was seen to shudder in acute distaste. Finally, when the penis belonging to a black South African gold miner flashed onto the screen – and by all accounts it was a huge and magnificent organ – she could stand it no longer. She rose and rushed out of the lecture-hall, but before she reached the door, Dr Campbell's voice, quiet but penetrating, was heard in the pin-dropping silence.

'There's no hurry, my dear: the next plane to Johannesburg doesna leave till Monday!'

'What part of the human body is it which under certain conditions swells up to six times its normal size?' the doctor asked the anatomy class. He pointed to a girl and invited her to answer the question. The girl blushed and hid her face.

'It's the ... the ... p ... p ... the ...'

'Yes?' said the doctor, 'what is it?'

'I don't know,' said the girl.

'You don't know?' repeated the doctor severely.

'No, I swear I don't,' she said unhappily. The doctor pointed to a male student and asked him the question. The student rose to his feet: 'It's the pupil of the eye,' he said.

'Quite right,' said the doctor approvingly, and then he turned to the girl. 'Young lady, I have three things to say to you. One, you haven't done your homework. Two, you have an obscene mind. Three, when you get married you are going to be very disappointed.'

my analyst told me to go home and make love to myself, but I keep getting a headache

What does GAY stand for?
Got AIDS yet?

.

What do you get when you cross a lawyer with a homosexual?
Legal AIDS.

What is the magic property of AIDS?
It turns fruit into vegetables.

Sex in the Press

Mr Root said that although there might be evidence of pre-marital intercourse by young people, there was little to suggest that this pattern persisted after marriage.

The Times

One evening when my mother called to return my house-key she found my husband making love to me as we didn't hear her let herself in. Now she won't speak to me. What can I do?

Letter in *Woman's Own*

Bedside Sex

EIGHTH ARMY PUSH BOTTLES UP GERMAN ARMY

Headline in the *New Chronicle*

To Mrs Smythe, wife of Mr G. F. A. Smythe (Reproduction and Distribution Department), a son Michael on April 10th.

British Council Staff Bulletin

Where the bee fucks there fuck I
In the cowflipf bell I lie . . .

Shakespeare: Davenant's edition of
The Tempest, published in 1678

Pupils at Stanground School, a mixed comprehensive near Peterborough, were warned yesterday about kissing and cuddling in the playground. A school spokesman said afterwards that any form of physical contact between the sexes could be construed in law as an indecent assault.

Guardian

She said the board had seen a film called *The Girl Traders*. It had originally been called *The White Slavers* and the board asked that the original title should be restored in case people thought it might be about girls going into business.

The Times

'We are really disturbed at the high number of indecent exposures, particularly at this time of the year. They are usually warm weather offences,' said Chief Inspector Wesley Watkins.

Nuneaton Evening Tribune

Bedside Sex

The magazine *Race Today* complains that British Airways are advertising flights to South Africa with a seductive picture of a beautiful black girl. Any white man following up this 'promise of unbounded sexuality', the magazine says, would get six months under the Immorality Acts. British Airways are unrepentant. 'Our poster for East Africa shows an elephant,' said their spokesman, 'but we are not suggesting . . . !'

The Times

Soon shalt thou hear the Bridegroom's voice
The midnight cry, 'behold I come!'

The Public School Hymn Book

Fashionable Chiswick Village, mod. con. flat cent. heat., set in attractive grounds with trees (tenants have their own private parts) . . .

Sunday Times

My husband and I offer our grateful thanks to the people of New Zealand for their present to our son the Prince of Wales of this totem-pole. This truly magnificent erection shall be placed in the gardens of Buckingham Palace for all to see and admire . . .

Reported in a New Zealand paper

Bedside Sex

In the *Girl's Own Paper* of 6 April 1907, there is a picture of a man and a girl gazing intently into each other's eyes. The title of the story to which it is an illustration is 'A Girl Without A Penny' and the caption underneath the picture – and it is plainly the girl who is speaking – is 'I swear I will not rest until I have found your Dick.'

Mr Mervyn Griffith-Jones, prosecuting counsel opposing the application, said 'It's a perfectly ordinary little case of a man charged with gross indecency with six guardsmen.'

Guardian

PRINCIPAL HORN, to lead enlarged section, good position.

Advertisement from Scottish National Orchestra

I was interested to learn in the *Mirror* that the Greeks have been accusing the English of being a race of homosexuals. Have the Greeks forgotten that the practice of homosexuality was brought into the Western world by the ancient Greeks themselves? If they disapprove of Vassall they have only themselves to blame.

Letter in the *Daily Mirror*

Sex in the Press

Sometime in the 1920s it was announced in *The Times* that Lord Berners, who liked men, was engaged to be married to his dear friend, Violet Trefusis, who preferred ladies. Lord Berners sent this disclaimer to *The Times*. 'Lord Berners wishes it to be known that he has departed from Lesbos and intends to spend the rest of his life on the Isle of Man.'

STEEL RISES TO BE FOUGHT VIGOROUSLY

Headline in *The Times*

LOT IN SODOM, the great American homosexual classic, and TEA FOR TWO.

Cinema poster

10.50 Epilogue. The Ten Commandments. Thou shalt not Commit Adultery (for details see pages 17 and 18).

Radio Times

DENTIST FILLS THE WRONG CAVITY

Headline in an American newspaper over a dentist on a rape charge

Bedside Sex

Royal Opera House Covent Garden

The Rape of
THE SLEEPING BEAUTY
Fonteyn, Nureyev

Daily Telegraph

Sex in the Press

The BOAC airline magazine, *Horizon*, reported that a couple had sexual intercourse on a New York–Sydney flight in full view of the other passengers. They had initially been sitting six rows apart and had been strangers.

> Come sit with me and be my Love
> And we will very quickly prove
> That earthly pleasure's no less sweet
> When done at thirty thousand feet.
>
> Our deft performance in mid-air
> May make our fellow travellers stare
> But hungry yearnings of the heart
> Can't be assuaged six rows apart.
>
> The safety-belts we wear shall be
> No guardians of our chastity
> We'll leave no act of love undone
> My dear, on Flight Five-Ninety-One.
>
> Where there's a will, we'll find a way
> To synchronize our ETA
> No one who sees us will deny
> It is the only way to fly.
>
> Thus shall our minds and bodies blend
> Till we have reached our journey's end
> And so, until they make us move,
> Come sit with me and be my Love.

Roger Woddis (after Marlowe), *New Statesman*

Bedside Sex

SEX LIFE RUINED BY POST OFFICE

Headline in the *Evening Standard*

DISGUSTING SCENES IN STRIP CLUB. VICAR ACTS

Headline of the year in a
Shropshire newspaper

Sex in the Press

COUNCILLOR FIGHTS ERECTION ON FOLLY BRIDGE

Headline in Oxford newspaper

A Cypriot who admitted shooting another man in the region of his sexual organs was given a two-year suspended sentence yesterday at the Old Bailey. Mr Justice Melford Stevenson told him: 'I bear in the forefront of my mind the fact that you come of a people who are prone to emotional storms, and who do dangerous things sometimes under the pressure of great emotions.'

Guardian

I always have mine
set on indecent
exposure

Bedside Sex

One of the reasons why the prison influence is so bad is because it is a homosexual community. Long ago it occurred to me that the atmosphere could be usefully moderated by introducing women of the right kind in male institutions to perform appropriate tasks.

Guardian

A leading American lecturer on medical ethics in Limerick yesterday said that uncontrolled sex could do only harm to the quality of human life and it was only by being responsible that one could learn to be responsible and that only by being disciplined that one could be disciplined. Dr Anthony Iezzi was speaking at Laurel Hill Convent in Limerick and his audience consisted of more than a hundred nuns and priests.

Cork Examiner

CHICK-SEXER WITH TWO FALSE LEGS SUED FOR BIGAMY

Headline in *News of the World*

When you marry your mistress, you create a job vacancy

Anonymous, from a Sunday newspaper

Why did Hitler act as he did? What was the secret of his power? At last we know the answer! Now the psychiatrists, led by Dr Walter Langer in his book *The Mind of Hitler* (Secker and Warburg, £3), step into the breach.

The results are predictable. Hitler's problem (like yours and mine) was sex. He was unable, as Dr Langer elegantly puts it, to 'derive sexual gratification' except 'from the act of having a woman urinate or defecate on him'. This was his 'masochistic perversion', the psychological consequence of his 'defective genitals' for Hitler suffered from the condition of monorchism or cryptorchism − in plain English, one of his testicles was missing or had failed to descend. In addition he underwent a rigorous toilet training which is 'the basis of a sadistic character'. Add, for good measure, an Oedipus complex and the fascinating sight of his parents copulating in bed and you have the recipe for a dictator.

Those who like this sort of thing, and doubtless there are many, are welcome to it. If, as we used to be told, Cleopatra's nose sealed the fate of empires, why should not Hitler's missing testicle have performed a similar historical function?

Geoffrey Barraclough, *Guardian*

Two headlines once appeared very close together in an issue of a popular Sunday newspaper:

CHURCH CONDEMNS ARTIFICIAL INSEMINATION . . .
    . . . FUCHS IS HERE TO STAY

Sex and the Single Pope

Oh Lord, please make me chaste – but not just yet!

St Augustine

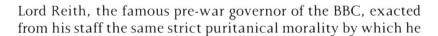

Lord Reith, the famous pre-war governor of the BBC, exacted from his staff the same strict puritanical morality by which he ordered his own life. One day he visited one of his senior announcers in his office and caught him *in flagrante delicto* with his secretary. Furious and outraged, he sacked the offending announcer. The announcer was very popular amongst his colleagues and a deputation of them went to Reith begging for his reinstatement. Reith finally relented. 'Verra well,' he said, 'he can come back, but he'll nae read the Epilogue.'

A nun goes to the Mother Superior and confesses that she is pregnant. 'Who's done this terrible thing, child?' she says angrily.

'That's all right,' says the nun consolingly, ''twas St Michael himself.'

'Nonsense, child, whatever made you think it was St Michael?'

'Aaaah sure, didn't I see it on the back of his underpants?'

An Englishman was in Dublin and attempted to buy a contraceptive unaware that this was strictly forbidden in Ireland. The chemist sternly refused to serve him. Outside, the Englishman was accosted by a very friendly Guard. 'I couldn't help overhearing what you was saying, sorr,' he said. 'An' I think I can help ye. Take the 78 bus to Dalkey and then a green-line coach to Tipperary. Get off at the Sacred Heart convent and take the path behind St Catherine's church. Cross the bridge over the stream and then over the field and you'll see Ryan's farm. Cross the field behind the farm and you'll see a little cowshed. Behind this you'll see a rainwater tank, and inside there's a metal box and inside that I think you'll find what you're looking for. But for pity's sake, sir, when you've finished with them be sure to put them back because they belong to the Dublin Football Team.'

The trouble with Paddy is
he's got no sense of
rhythm

Sex and the Single Pope

A newsreader in the Vatican Radio service broadcasting to the French colonies meant to say *'la population immense du Cape'*, but instead committed the greatest spoonerism in broadcasting – not to say papal – history when he said *'la copulation immense du Pape'*.

A nun went to Reverend Mother and confessed that she was pregnant. 'Go to the kitchen,' she was told, 'and drink a bottle of vinegar and the juice of five lemons.'

'But that won't get rid of the baby,' said the nun in surprise.

'It won't,' said Reverend Mother grimly, 'but at least it'll take that smug smile off your face.'

The late Evelyn Waugh, a Catholic writer, once attempted to explain to the late Victor Gollancz, a Jewish publisher, the Church's teaching on the subject of death-bed repentance. 'If you make an act of perfect contrition before you die, then you will eventually go to heaven, no matter how sinful your life has been,' he said.

Gollancz was politely incredulous. 'Do you mean to tell me that if a man was committing what you Catholics call the mortal sin of fornication and died of a heart attack while he was enjoying his climax, all he needs to enjoy eternal bliss is to say he's sorry as long as he manages to get it in before his heart gives out . . . is this *really* what you Catholics believe and teach?'

Evelyn Waugh nodded. 'Yes,' he said, 'but it must be a really perfect act of contrition, he must be sincerely sorry.'

'Supposing it wasn't perfect?' asked Gollancz. 'Supposing he was only pretending to be sorry. Would he then go to hell?'

'Yes, I suppose he would,' replied Waugh, and it was this conversation which inspired Gollancz to write the following limerick:

> Whilst engaged in his final emission,
> Evelyn Waugh's soul flew off to perdition.
> It wasn't the * * * *
> Which inspired this bad luck
> But an act of *imperfect* contrition.

The teacher was instructing a class of boys about the Immaculate Conception, informing them that this was God's special and unique gift of Grace to Mary's soul, the Virgin Birth being an added gift to her body. She then asked: 'What is the difference between the Immaculate Conception and the Virgin Birth?' and a swift answer came from a boy in the front row: 'Nine months!'

It's a strange irony that when the Pope has made a definite ruling against the use of the Pill or any other form of birth control, the name of the leading Catholic newspaper should be the *Tablet*.

Why does the Pope always wear swimming trunks in his bath?

Because he hates to look down on the unemployed.

The priest preached a very strong sermon on the importance of regular sexual relations for married couples. Paddy and Kathleen listened with great interest. 'Paddy,' she whispered to him after the priest had finished, 'do we have sexual relations?' Paddy grinned happily. 'Sure we do,' he replied. 'Then it's funny we don't hear from them,' said Kathleen, puzzled and unhappy, 'not even a card at Christmas.'

What is the Catholic definition of a contraceptive?

Something which a Protestant uses on every conceivable occasion.

Sex and the Single Pope

A Catholic journalist interviewed the Mother Superior of an Italian convent and questioned her about her wartime experiences. 'The Fascists were beasts, beasts my son. You won't believe it, but they broke into the convent and raped every nun, except Sister Mary Anita. Not that the Germans were any better – same story, every nun was raped, except Sister Mary Anita . . . and the Americans: disgusting brutes they were, every nun raped without mercy except Sister Mary Anita.'

'What's the matter with Sister Mary Anita?' said the journalist in surprise.

'Aaaah, my son,' replied the Mother Superior, 'she's not keen on that sort of thing.'

'Father,' said the youth in the confessional, 'I want to confess to the sin of nail biting.' The priest shook his head reassuringly. 'That's not a sin, my son,' he said. 'Don't you know that nail biting is only a substitute for masturbation?' The youth was deeply shocked by this. 'But Father,' he said sternly, 'there is *no* substitute for masturbation.'

A nun went to Reverend Mother and said she wished to become a prostitute. Reverend Mother screamed and fainted. When she returned to consciousness she asked weakly, 'What did you say you wanted to be?'

'A prostitute.'

'That's all right,' said Reverend Mother smiling in relief, 'for a terrible moment I thought you said a *Protestant*.'

Bedside Sex

'Father, is it a sin to sleep with a girl?

'Not exactly,' replied the priest, 'but you young fellers, you don't sleep.'

I thought celibate was what we ate on Fridays

A young Catholic farmer married a Protestant girl and after she had given him a son he converted her to the Faith. He was middle-aged when she died so he married another Protestant girl who, after giving him a son, was converted to the Faith and later died. By this time he was getting on in years and again married a Protestant girl, but after a year she was not only not pregnant but not Catholic either. So the priest goes down to see him. 'Patrick,' he says, 'I have put up with your marrying all these Protestant girls because you convert them fairly fast but it doesn't seem to be working out with the latest one. What's the trouble?'

'Well, Father,' he replies, with more than a touch of embarrassment, 'I'm getting old and the old converter ain't what it used to be.'

Sex in Miscellany

What do girls say after sex? Depends on their nationality:

The American girl: Hey, that was great – but what did you say your name was?

The German girl: Ach, so, that was wunderbar. Now we shall eat.

The Russian girl: That was a vital and significant contribution to the Five Year Plan, comrade. Now I must go and oil my tractor.

The English girl: Darling, that was absolutely marvellous. I must go and tell mummy.

Two Welsh miners, Dai and his friend, Morgan, are killed in a pit accident. Dai is a good boy and goes to heaven, but Morgan is a bad boy and had spent his life chasing girls and so he goes to hell. After a million years in heaven, Dai gets bored and asks permission to go down to hell and visit Morgan to see how he is getting on. He is shown into a splendid room; there is a table piled high with food and drink and a large bed covered with beautiful naked girls. Morgan is sitting in the middle looking very bored and unhappy.

'Doing all right, boyo,' says Dai in surprise, but Morgan sighs deeply and shakes his head.

'It's sheer bloody hell, I'm telling you,' he moans.

Dai shrugs his shoulders in bewilderment and goes to the drink table and helps himself to a beer. But he can't pour it out because the top is stopped with solid glass. 'That's funny,' he said, 'none of these beer bottles have holes in them.'

Morgan sighs deeply and looks at all the girls. 'I told you it was hell.'

A chap takes a girl to his room to see his etchings; they land up in bed. Afterwards he says: 'I'm sorry . . . if I'd known you were a virgin I'd have been more gentle.' She says: 'Blimey, if I'd known you were going to be gentle, I'd have taken me tights orf.'

From the Rules of Contract Bridge:

FORCING PRINCIPLE. This is used to produce game where partner, though possessing game requirements, fails through timidity or inexperience. Forcing occasions are when:

1. Partner has great honour strength and refuses to open
2. You possess length or a freak
3. Partner has a complete bust and you hold no stoppers.

Further rules governing the forcing principle are:

1. Never leave your partner with an unguarded major
2. Never employ the forcing principle without first considering the result obtained by careful manipulation of the hand.

LEADS STRONG AND WEAK. When a partner leads the queen up to your jack, it is a strength lead. When partner holds queen in hand after the jack is exposed, it is a weakness lead.

TAKE-OUT. A regulation take-out can be made to prolong the game or to permit the partner to pass. An immediate take-out is essential if partner is vulnerable. A forced take-out is the result of being caught in a minor. A jump take-out is advisable when there is a danger of losing the rubber.

NO-BID RESPONSE. Can range from a shapeless bust to a raised point. This is effective after the partner has opened his rubber and rises in his suit. The hand pattern is likely to determine which suit is opened when there is a wide choice . . .

It's no good, Mr Ormsby-Gore,
I shan't sleep with you any more,
You're all of a sweat
And you haven't come yet,
And *look* at the time – half past four!

A gentleman should always know the name of the girl he slept with the night before.

Who are the four most important men in a girl's life?

1. The Doctor who says, 'Please lie down.'
2. The Dentist who says, 'Open wide, please.'
3. The Coalman who says, 'Do you want it back or front?'
4. The Banker who says, 'When you take it out you lose interest.'

Two Australians, Bob and Jack, are digging for gold in the bush and suddenly Bob is bitten on the penis by a snake. Jack immediately phones the radio doctor. 'Doc,' he says, 'my mate's been bitten on the penis by a snake – what shall I do?' The doctor says: 'You gotta suck out the poison or he's only got two minutes to live.' Jack replaces the receiver in alarm. Bob, still writhing and twisting in agony, turns to him. 'What does he say, sport?' Jack looks at him sadly. 'He says you only got two minutes to live.'

The Post Office would appear to be the last place where you would expect to find sexual humour but one must never underrate the influence of bureaucracy. The following are authentic extracts from letters addressed by postal employees to the Welfare Department:

1. I cannot get sick pay. I have children, can you tell me why this is?
2. Mrs Smith has had no clothes for a year and has been regularly visited by th clergy.
3. Sir, I am forwarding my marriage certificate and two children one of which as you will see is a mistake.
4. In answer to your letter I have given birth to a boy, weighing ten pounds. I hope this is satisfactory.
5. Please send my money at once. I need it badly. I have fallen into errors with my landlord.
6. In accordance with your instructions, I have given birth to twins in the enclosed envelope.
7. I want my money as quickly as you can send it. I have been in bed with the doctor for a week and he doesn't seem to be doing much good. And if things don't improve I shall have to get another doctor.

Two old ladies were watching a hippopotamus being fed in the zoo. One of them asked the keeper, 'Is that a lady or a gentleman hippopotamus?' The keeper was very shocked by this. 'That, madam,' he said firmly, 'is a question which should only interest another hippopotamus!'

André Maurois

A man goes up to a girl at a party. 'Will you?' he asks. And she says: 'You've talked me into it.'

Tattooed across a prostitute's abdomen:

PAY AS YOU ENTER

Tattooed across the buttocks of a male prostitute with a theatrical clientele:

ENTREE DES ARTISTES

They say that after you've been with one, you never want to go with a white one again.

Bedside Sex

For what did Venus love Adonis?
But for the gristle, where no bone is.

A famous judge, known for his wit and cynicism, once gave an unfavourable verdict on a case whose accused was black. The accused, disgusted with the turn of events, showed his contempt for the court by dropping his trousers and pants and exposing his virility. The judge looked at him and turned to his usher, saying, '*In this court, two black balls means exclusion.*'

An actor went out with a tart,
Whose method was subtle but smart.
   She rehearsed him in bed,
   But wished she were dead
On learning the length of his part.

There were once two young people of taste,
Who were beautiful down to the waist,
   So they limited love
   To the regions above
And thus remained perfectly chaste.

A man persuades a girl to come back to his flat. 'I must warn you that I'm in the menopause', she said. 'That's all right,' he said, 'I'll follow in the Aston Martin.'

He reached his room to find three other boys busily engaged in abusing their housemaster. They took no notice of John who leaned against the wall.

Vachell, *The Hill*

A lesbian from Khartoum,
Invited a queer to her room.
　　She said 'Now, my dear,
　　Let's get this quite clear.
Who does what and with which and to whom?'

*

She had the shy, modest, virginal, sexless look of the professional nymphomaniac.

THE PORTIONS OF THE FEMALE

The portions of the female
Which appeal to man's depravity
Are fashioned with particular care
And what at first appears to be
A modest little cavity
Is really an elaborate affair.
Now doctors who have studied these
Most feminine phenomena
With numerous experimental dames

Bedside Sex

Have taken all the items
Of the Gentle Sex's abdomena
And given them some charming Latin names.
There's the *vulva*, the *vagina*,
And of course the *perineum*,
And the *hymen* that is often
Found in Brides,
And there's lots of little things
You'd love 'em, if you could see 'em,
The *clitoris* and God knows what besides.
What a pity it is then
When we common people chatter

Who do you think
about?

Boy George

Of those mysteries to which I have referred.
And we use for such a
delicate
and complicated matter,
Such a very short
and ugly
little word.

This is anonymous but tradition has it that it was written by
A. P. Herbert during an unusually long and tedious session in
the House of Commons.

What do a spider's web and a passionate kiss have in common?
Both lead to the undoing of a fly.

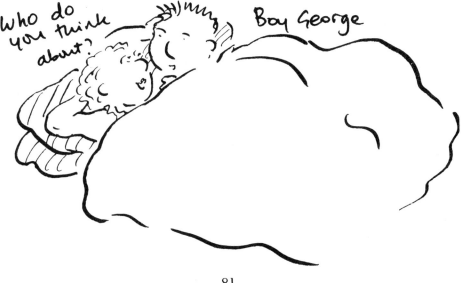

'Definitions' is a popular party game. Here are a few which I have discovered.

Fellatio is the love that dare not speak its name because its mouth is always full.

Masturbation is the working man's television.

Nudists are people who wear one-button suits.

Incest is a game for the whole family.

Cunnilingus is the new Irish airline.

Genitalia: the new Italian airline.

Ballroom dancing is the vertical expression of a horizontal desire.

A Virgin is a rookie-nookie.

Rape is (1) pressing an unwanted gift on a stranger; (2) attacking with a friendly weapon.

Lesbianism is two hers making a him (hymn) without an organ.

❧

Did you ever hear about Morgan, the young Welsh homosexual? He was sent to Ireland as a suitable treat for Casement.

Sex in Miscellany

Overheard in a Cardiff bus:

1st WOMAN: Did you hear about Maggie Jones?
2nd WOMAN: No, what's she done?
1st WOMAN: Getting married, she is.
2nd WOMAN: I didn't know she was pregnant.
1st WOMAN: She isn't.
2nd WOMAN: Getting married and not pregnant? Oh, there's posh for you.

Ken Tynan speaking of a very uxorious playwright:

'He puts his talent into his work and his genius into his wife.'

Man goes to a party alone, leaving his wife behind. They play party games and the game is that he must speak on a subject which is taken out of a hat: he has to speak on sex. When he gets back home he has to give an account of the evening but he tells his wife that the subject he had to speak about was yachting. Next day, she meets a woman in the supermarket who was at the party.

'Your husband was a scream last night,' she said, 'he spoke for over an hour on his subject and he was very funny.'

'Can't think how,' said the wife. 'He's only done it twice. First time his hat fell off and the next time he fell into the water.'

Cardew Robinson

Bedside Sex

Four jokes from Richard Lamb's uniquely pornographic repertoire:

We're going to a gang-bang, my brother and me,
It's with a girl, and it's all for free.
We're going to wear our boots and jeans,
And stuff her fanny with Heinz Baked Beans.
　　　(. . . We were going to fuck her but it doesn't rhyme . . .)

　　　　　A jingle you've not heard on TV and possibly never will.

MP's wife (on their wedding night): 'Would the Conservative member like to stand for election, there has been a split in the Conservative ranks.'
　　MP (disgruntled): 'The member did stand an hour ago but lost his deposit.'

Gorilla forces his way into bedroom, throws husband out of bed and grabs the wife. She screams for help. The husband merely says, 'tell him you have a headache.'

Father to his teenage son: 'Well, boy, time you and me had a little talk about sex.'
Son (chirpily): 'Okay, dad, what is it you want to know?'

John Crosby gleefully quoted this ancient joke as being the first such he'd ever heard:

She: 'Hey, quit this fooling and take your finger out.'
He (chuckling horribly): 'I'm not fooling, sister, and this ain't my finger.'

84

A group of German women during the war were asked to name their favourite men:

The first said, 'Hitler, because he is so magnetic.'

The second said, 'Goering because he is so handsome and well-covered.'

The third said, 'Goebbels because he is so clever.'

And the fourth said, 'Winston Churchill, because he has just said over the radio that it would be long and hard and stiff and there would be no withdrawal!'

Did you ever hear the one about the newly weds who didn't know the difference between Vaseline and putty? Their windows all fell out.

Golf would appear to be a very obscene and disgusting game, as can be judged from a report taken from a popular Sunday paper:

Brian Huggett took his niblick firmly in both hands and birdied round the fourteenth hole. 'I rammed in a five-footer on the first, a fifteen-footer on the third and a thirty-five-footer for the fourth,' he said. 'The pin placings were diabolical. I shortened my grip and put a bit more weight on the left foot and just eased it in. It was a case of safety first. I just concentrated on aiming for the safe side of the hole. Get on the wrong side and you could slide it eight foot past.' He played safe on the eighteenth too, pulling away from his putt to call to the gallery, 'What's the best score in?' Reassured, he banged his putt straight in.

The Family Planning Association has issued an information bulletin on how people first learned about sex. The letter accompanying it says: 'It contains a wealth of useful facts and figures, some of which I hope you will consider worthy of reproduction.'

If you go to sleep with your problem in your hand, you will find the solution on your stomach in the morning.

Ancient Tibetan proverb

Errol Flynn acquired a niche in the history of St Paul's School by being publicly birched and expelled for impregnating the High Master's daughter: this could be called a case of dishonourable discharge.

She goes about using sex as a sort of *shrimping net*.

Noel Coward, *Hay Fever*

> Houdini was born prematurely
> Of this I have no doubt.
> I spoke to his mother and father,
> Who said 'He found a way out.'

Bedside Sex

There are fairies at the bottom of my garden
That used to worry hell out of me.
But now the government has made it legal
I've invited them all home for tea.

Drink to me only with thine eyes,
They are so full of laughter.
But when she tries to mesmerize
I know what she's really after.

When Mae West said to the Invisible Man, 'Come up and see me sometime,' the answer was: 'Thanks, honey, I've already been.'

The quickest quickie . . . 'It won't hurt you – did it?'

Did you ever hear the story of the two Australian sheepfarmers working on a very remote outpost? They were found guilty.

By a computer they were dated
Their bodies auto-mated

And two became one.
But their output was none
Because his input was false
So their second divorce
Which leaves them free
For computer date three.

Lechery . . . drink doth stimulate the desire but spoils the performance . . .

The Porter, *Macbeth*

A teenage boy was going through all the agonies of his first love affair, and in despair he appealed to his aged ninety-year-old grandmother. 'Gran,' he said, 'how old do you have to be before you are released from the sufferings of unsatisfied sexual appetites?'

The old woman gazed into the flickering fire for a very long time and finally she gave her answer. 'I don't know.'

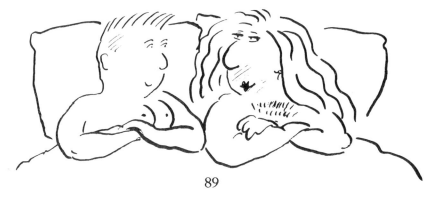

Paddy went to a shop and bought himself a pair of wellington boots. But they didn't fit so he went to the shop to complain. 'They don't fit because you've got them on the wrong feet,' said the shop manager. 'I'll tell you what I'll do. I'll put a big letter L for the left foot and an R for the right foot.'

'That's wonderful,' exclaimed Paddy. 'And you managed to explain something which has been bothering me for a long time. My wife has a pair of knickers with C and A on them.'

How do you play African roulette?

You lie down naked on your back in the middle of the village square and twelve African women take it in turns to give you oral sex. But one of them is a cannibal.

A ventriloquist travelling through a very remote part of the country stopped at a lonely farm and asked to see round. As the farmer was showing him the horses he thought he'd have some fun so proceeded to make one of them talk. The farmer rushed in panic to his wife. 'Betty, those animals are talking. If that stupid horse says anything about me, it's a bloody lie.'

Man goes into general shop and buys a packet of Tampax. The manager offers him a lawnmower as well. 'Why should I need a lawnmower?' he asks in surprise.

'Well, your weekend's been fucked up,' said the manager, 'you might as well mow the lawn.'

Sex in Miscellany

The Greek had been happily married for a year. One day he said to his wife, 'Tonight when we have sex, let's do it a different way. Turn over.' She shook her head. 'No,' she said firmly, 'that way I get pregnant.'

In his last year Edward VII paid a final visit to his mistress of many years, Lillie Langtry. He walked round the house he had bought her, looking nostalgically at all the priceless furniture, carpets, antiques, pictures and clothes and jewels. 'My God, Lillie,' he said. 'I've spent enough on you to sink a battleship.'

Her reply is her only recorded witticism: 'You've spent enough *inside* me to float one.'

Shortly before her marriage, Grace Kelly attended a rehearsal of *Othello* at the Dublin Theatre Festival, in which Mícheál MacLiammóir – one of Ireland's most famous and greatly loved homosexuals – was playing Iago. The dialogue went roughly as follows:

Mícheál: Do you wish you were back in the theatre, my dear?
Grace Kelly (dreamily): Oh y-e-e-es. Sometimes I lie awake at night and say to myself, some day a wonderful script will land on my bed and I can make a comeback.
Mícheál (smiling approvingly): I know exactly what you mean, my dear. Sometimes *I* lie awake at night and say to myself, some day *my* prince will come . . .

At a lecture on population, the lecturer explained that every

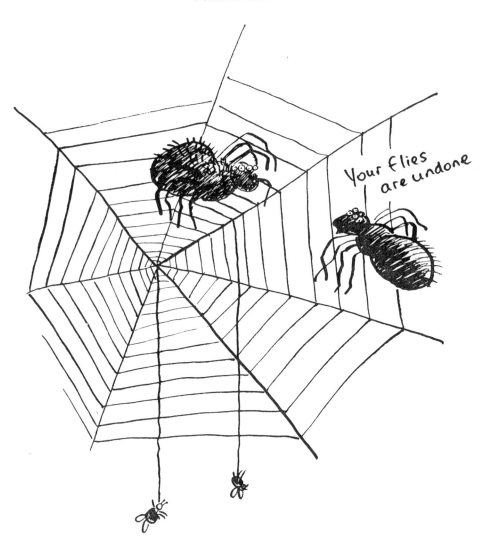

four seconds a woman gives birth to a baby. A man in the crowd yelled out: 'We oughta find this woman and stop her.'

'Hello, is that the Salvation Army?'
'Yes it is.'
'Is it true that you save fallen women?'
'Yes, we do.'
'Good. Will you save me two for Saturday night?'

A social worker put a question to a Mexican, an Englishman and a Greek. 'What is your attitude towards women?'

The Mexican says, 'A women is like a bowl of hot chilli and beans, something to be enjoyed and then forgotten.'

The Englishman says, 'She is like a book, to be taken down from the shelf, dusted, read, and then placed back on the shelf for next time.'

The Greek says, 'A woman is like a long-playing record. You play first one side and then you turn it over and play the other.'

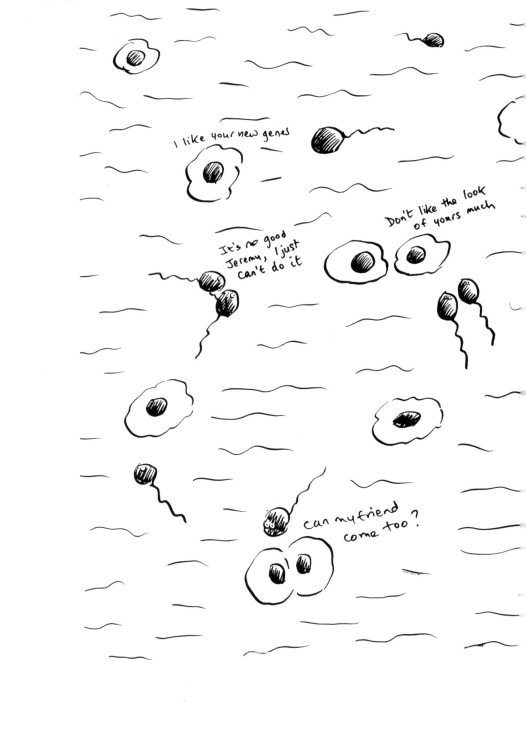

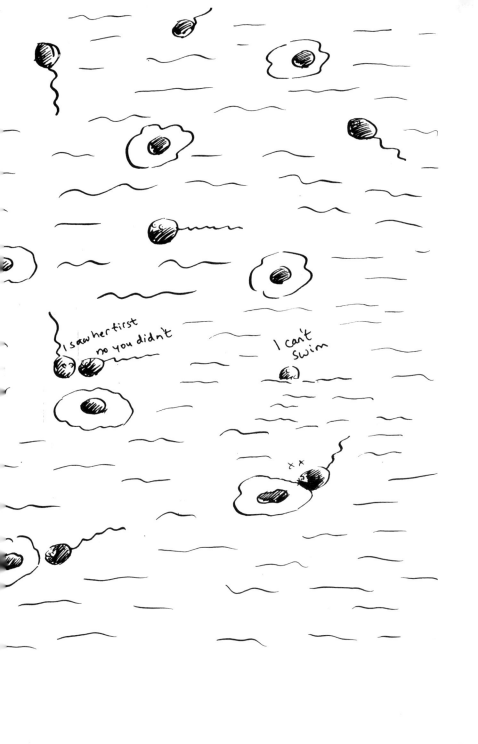